CHICAGO YESTERDAY

Published by GINGKO PRESS Inc.
5768 Paradise Drive, Suite J, Corte Madera, CA 94925, USA
Phone (415) 924–9615, Fax (415) 924–9608
email Gingko@linex.com
Copyright © English Edition 1998

3–927258–69-5

"Chicago Yesterday – Leben in den 20er und 30er Jahren"
First published 1998 by Kunstverlag Weingarten, Germany
Copyright © 1998 Kunstverlag Weingarten GmbH

← Twilight sinks over the gigantic Wrigley Building complex and the constant growing number of skyscrapers
on both sides of the river

CHICAGO

YESTERDAY

Gingko Press
Corte Madera, California
1998

Chicago's "Twin Building" or Wrigley Building towers over Michigan Avenue. The chewing gum giant commissioned in 1924 this architectural icon – one of the finest architectural structures in the country.

INTRODUCTION

FIRST IMPRESSIONS

This collection of photographs shows Chicago as it looked when I first explored it with my grandfather in the early thirties. He was a businessman, with very little business to do after the stock market crash of 1929. He was also a gregarious man who loved the diverse life of the city.

To fill the day he would take me to his office, where I could play with pens, ink, and other 'adult' toys. After an hour or so, with the day's work done, we would stroll through Chicago's famous Loop district, investigating any mysterious areas and or activities that we happened upon. We examined construction projects and explored office buildings, hotels and rail terminals. We made regular rounds of shops and outdoor markets and viewed the intense bargaining which, in those humbling times, only rarely concluded with a sale.

We lunched on a variety of exotic foods, which were probably not suitable for either of us.

The city offered many varieties of "theater": trial court, a political rally, funerals, weddings, and naturally baseball and movies.

It seemed that everything was possible in my Chicago, and if my grandfather had his doubts about the matter, he never let on.

THE REAL WORLD

My boyish optimism regarding the city notwithstanding, Chicago's actual prospects were less encouraging. In fact, during the early thirties Chicago was stopped dead in its tracks. Unemployment was rampant and 'normal', with no improvement in sight (except for those who believed President Roosevelt could work miracles). Looking at the photographs, one is surprised to see how rather well dressed we were at the beginning of the Great Depression. Perhaps we were too occupied or oblivious to dress properly for the disaster.

Our new consumer products and goods that were shown during the 'Century of Progress' exhibition at the lakefront didn't really seem to be intended for the visitors of that fair. They were after all not fools, and knew there was no money. The 'wonders of tomorrow' that were displayed at this exposition could not possibly have beeen distributed. But one didn't let this fact interfere with 'the show'. They couldn't dance like Fred Astaire either. The coming war which would eventually reinvigorate our economy was still a very small cloud on a distant horizon.

In terms of planning and architecture, Chicago in 1930 was at the end of its fourth stage of development.

GEOGRAPHY AS DESTINY

Chicago's growth was inevitable due to its location. The site had already been a native trading center long before the first French explorers arrived. It straddled a low continental divide between two important river systems, the St. Lawrence and the Mississippi. Eventually, a connecting canal and port were built. When rail finally replaced water in the transportation of people and goods, Chicago became the hub of the nation. Lake Michigan acted as a continental barrier, forcing all traffic through the same site.

The first European settlement, dating back to the 1830's, was no more than a collection of cheap, wooden structures built with the balloon frame system. This required unskilled labor to nail together light wooden frames that supported a thin diaphragm enclosure. The balloon frame system allowed a town to be built in just a few days.

Balloon framing was appropriate for sparsely settled villages but tended to burn easily, and so did not last long in densely populated areas. The central area burned in the devastating Chicago Fire of 1873 had been a temporary camp composed largely of these structures.

THE FIRST CHICAGO 'SCHOOL'

During the difficult period after the fire (1873), and before the Chicago Colombian Exposition (1893) the city was rebuilt with more permanent materials. Where European stylistic precedents existed, they were employed in classical buildings such as the Library and in the Gothic quadrangles of the University of Chicago.

However, it was in the Loop, Chicago's central commercial district, that a new chapter in architectural history was being written. High land values led to high densities. The streets became increasingly crowded and noisy. Office buildings were crowded together and shot upward seeking daylight and fresh air.

These high rise lofts were little more than thinly decorated metal frames for which the elevators provided

The "Lindbergh", a blinking light installed atop a new skyscraper, was named after the first pilot to cross the Atlantic.

access, as they do for workers in mine shafts. Modern office buildings were utilitarian structures with few aesthetic pretensions. Nothing in architectural history suggested an approach for their design. Only the architects who were designing them conceived them as art.

The city's social and political leaders, looking to Europe for the finer things, were not concerned about the appearance of these buildings beyond their practical value, and considered the city to be a form of industrial pollution, there to capitalize on its commercial center and its mines, mills and stockyards.

It is therefore not surprising that this impressive collection of photographs shows none of the earlier buildings, although Chicago's architectural reputation is ultimately based on them.

Richardson, Jenney, Adler and Sullivan, Burnham and Root, Holabird and Roche, and Frank Lloyd Wright were not felt to be worth mentioning back in 1930. It would take a second generation of European modernists to find the aesthetic vitality and beauty in the new American metropolis.

THE SECOND WAVE

The buildings included in this book are large corporate projects, produced by a generation of well organized, commercial architectural and engineering firms which emerged in the years after the Colombian Exposition (1893), but which disappeared in the Great Depression (1929). The owners of these buildings were companies rather than individuals. The designers who were college-trained in accepted European styles also worked in collaboration with firms whose mentality was to discourage individual expression. This combined aesthetic had much in common with the later work of Soviet architects in the Stalin period.

There are fortunately other areas of the city where commercial structures tended to form urban spaces of startling beauty. The best of these extravagant environments is well illustrated in a number of these photographs. The Michigan Avenue Bridge adjacent to the Tribune Tower, the Medinah Temple, Wrigley Building, London Guarantee Building, Mather Tower and 333 North Michigan are all in this area. We still have all these buildings, though some of the names have changed. They are a strange, almost naive assemblage of historic forms, but they happily come together around this natural, unplanned space with its double level street and bridge to form Chicago's unique civic plaza.

Toward the end of this period the Art Deco buildings

of John Root Jr. in the 1920's marked an escape from academic formulas and a return to the search for the perfect skyscraper. The Palmolive Building and 333 North Michigan Avenue are shown in several of these photographs. They remain today with much of our popular culture, as sophisticated artefacts from the jazz age – a happy, irresponsible and productive time that also contributed to Chicago's gangster mythology.

After the Second World War, Mies van der Rohe led Chicago on its third crusade in search of the perfect high rise tower. During the period covered in this book however, this movement had not yet crossed the Atlantic. They were just taking root in Germany.

OUR DAILY LIFE

The natural rhythms of Chicago life seem to be governed by the climate. Our weather changes continually. Every family has memories of unscheduled 'holidays' brought about by storms, floods, heat waves, or blizzards. Our great sweet lake occasionally grows playful and imitates the North Sea. We have a fine fire department and magnificent fires. Chicago dogs learn to sing to the sirens of emergency vehicles.

I am now about as old as my grandfather was back then, during those reminiscent early walks. I've had more opportunity to work than he, and have enjoyed the qualities of the city he taught me to see.

Chicago is not as hard as it was. The air is cleaner. We don't produce as much steel and heavy machinery. The cattle are gone, replaced by swarms of traders, lawyers and accountants. Michigan Avenue looks very respectable, with more varieties of food imaginable. But the elevated train over Wabash Avenue as noisy as when I was four.

We may have outgrown some of the enthusiasm for the future which so imbued us in those days. We have since lived the future that was promised by the 1933 World's Fair. It was not all bad, we gained in parking space what we lost in the rails.

A few years ago some of our civic leaders proposed that we have a third World's Fair, with a committee of distinguished architects to plan it. The preliminary drawings seemed to focus on the past, and not the future. Our expectations seem to decline. When the proposed World's Fair of 1993 was finally canceled, everyone seemed relieved.

Chicago is older now and more selective about progress.

John Hartray (Architect, Chicago)

↑ The elevated rail at Lake and Wells is the busiest crossing of its kind.

→ In 1928 Chicago was one of the largest cities in the USA, second only to New York, and modeled its Skyline in that city's image. The slender tower of the Mather building, seen here in the foreground, is prominent among an already formidable array of skyscrapers.

Michigan Avenue on a rainy night, the Wrigley Building in the rear left

Most architects relegate unsightly chimneys to an indiscernible place of their rooftops. The Wieboldt Hall of Commerce in Chicago appears to have no chimney at all. Yet it is there however where one may least suspect it, integrated into its 200 feet tower – a lovely piece of gothic architecture.

↑ Chicago's monumental Merchandise Mart, at the time the world's largest commercial space, was bathed in light in 1932. With its 600 floodlights reflected in the water this massive concrete block was transformed into a fairy like castle – a spectacular example of electrical illumination.

← Around a newly built highrise, a view of Chicago's central skyscraper district.

This too was Chicago. This little log cabin is located in Lincoln Park's bird sanctuary. No pedestrians are allowed. The only population here are the birds.

The towers of this colossal structure appear to be the entrance to a massive fortress. This perspective is lost however as an even larger structure was built across the street. The powerful effect of the two buildings, now facing each other, is that of a man-made canyon where the street runs.

↑ Chicago is the city of towers. The architecture recalls many periods and styles, from classic to modern.

← The snow, cold and haze have the Michigan Avenue highrises in their grip. The sun's meek effort to throw some light onto this bleak scene is in vain, as the wind brings forth yet another bank of clouds, and in a few minutes all will disappear among a blizzard.

The year is 1926. The automobile has triumphed and is not only a major factor in the life of the metropolis, but has brought new challenges to city-planners. Wacker Drive, the first split-level city highway in Chicago, opened to traffic. It was one of the first built in the USA.

The World's Fair is coming to town and Chicago readies its transformation for a new era. After years of pompous and monumental style building, Chicago turned in 1931 to the modern. On Northern Island we see the steel skeleton of the Electrical Building with its semi-circular court, built in the functional style of the day. Across the lagoon the Hall of Science the "heart of the exposition" next to the Soldier Field Museum and the Field Museum. In the distance the vanishing silhouette of the skyscrapers in the city haze.

In front of the Field Museum with its massive Doric temple front a train emerges from underground. Already in 1926 the city could no longer afford the daily transport of almost 5,000 truck loads of freight above ground. 61 miles of tunnels underneath the city were built to move millions of cubic yards of excavation from the new buildings, as well as goods to their destination per underground train cargo. The excavation was disposed as land fill south of Grant Park.

↑ In 1933 an estimated million Chicagoans lined the lake front from the Illinois Indiana Line to the Navy Pier in the heart of the city to cheer the arrival of General Italo Balbo and his trans-Atlantic fliers. The above photograph shows the Navy Pier where several hundred thousand assembled, as the last of the planes landed.

→ The Art Institute of Chicago. For the period a surprisingly well-proportioned and sober structure. Built to house the fine arts, the planners of this building achieved a perfect architectural unity for its purpose.

Polk Street at the intersection of Garibaldi Avenue on Chicago's West Side (1934) showing some of the buildings scheduled to be razed and replaced by model homes and apartments in a $12.5 million State project. Thirty-seven city blocks covering 160 acres, are to be entirely rebuilt.

↑ The Fine Arts Building in Jackson Park, which, during the Exposition of 1893 and for many years after, housed some of the world's finest works of art. In 1926 this last relic of the Exposition of 1893 is inhabited by thousands of pigeons. The contents of the building were moved to the New Field Museum in 1921 and the old building was closed to the public.

→ This 'eclectic' building has a little of everything, from Tudor to Disney to 20th century industrial style, something for everybody. Proportion and taste are neglected in the hustle and bustle of the turn-of-the-century. The return to taste emerged with the dawn of the Art Nouveau movement.

Chicago by night. A street in the city center between Randolph and Washington Street.

↑ On November 4, 1929, the most modern opera house in the world opened its doors in Chicago. When the Art Deco curtain was raised in front of the auditorium, 3,471 people saw the premiere of the Chicago Civic Opera. The building and its innovative technology cost twenty million dollars and was praised for its distinct beauty and exquisite design.

→ Luxury up to the highest balcony and an extravagant coffered ceiling. At the back of each of its panels is a cove conceiling the lighting and ventilating grills. The details reveal that money was no object when the Chicago Civic Opera was built.

In 1925 these firemen were the heroes, when it came to extinguish what foolishness, thoughtlessness or even purpose had set on fire. Gold medals were the fair reward for good deeds. Fire department chief Arthur Seyferlich obviously enjoys the burden of his duty: decorating the brave members of Hook and Ladder Truck No. 3.

Christmas time in Chicago, and the fire-proof plastic tree with its tiny colored bulbs has no chance against the wild plant from Northern Michigan. The first customers on North Clark Street come by to take theirs home and the children's eyes begin to shine.

Prohibition 1930. These cartons of fruit juice turned out to have strong traces of alcohol. The $75,000 stock of beer and liquor-making paraphernalia of the Grein & Pahls store on West Madison Street was seized on May 10th, 1930. Upholders of the law proudly present their bounty for the camera as the clerk makes his entry. Every bottle of beer and whiskey is destined for the gully. The other side of the coin: the Prohibition was largely responsible for bringing the Mafia in America to power.

Prohibition repealed. The popular German-American pub-owner Hermann Berghoff was the first man in America to receive a license to serve beer. On the upper-left of his licence, the number 1.

Rehearsal for Grandmothers Club revue. This group depicting the "Dionne Quintuplets and Doctor Dafoe" are rehearsing one of the acts for the Grandmothers Club revue under the title "Grandma's Scandals of 1939" in full regalia.

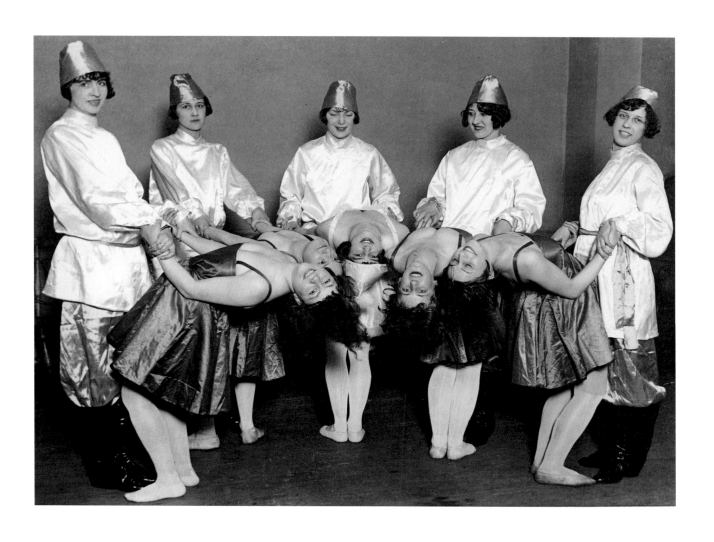

In 1926 the YWCA presented the winners of the poster competition for the annual benefit in Chicago. Gymnastics, swimming and dancing were among the disciplines these as yet undiscovered acrobats and athletes would take on.

Chicagoans showed up in droves and surrounded the Criminal Court to get a glimpse of Chicago's "Enemy No 1", the legendary gangleader Al Capone.

The largest transfer of the city's prisoners was completed on March 1st, 1929 when more than 1,370 "Jailbirds" were moved from their old cells to the new Bastille in Chicago. Each of the ten buses chartered for this special occasion were loaded with 39 prisoners accompanied by four policemen and two Deputy Sheriffs who rode inside, while four Motorcycle Cops and a detective squad escorted them. At the new jail 100 more Motorcycle Police remained on duty ready to take up a chase should any of the prisoners decide to seek freedom.

Frank Wilson, 22; Ed Wallace, 30; and Paul Keltner (left to right), are held by the Police in connection with the blast which wrecked the State Office Building in Columbus, Ohio, killing ten. Keltner was found in Chicago, while Wallace and Wilson were arrested entering Chicago in a stolen car. Wallace, a dynamite expert, had been working in a tunnel near the building when the blast occurred. A large quantity of explosives were found in the car.

↑ Russell Mossman, Wilson Herren and Earle Steele, better known in those days as "The Three Mustacheteers of the Air", at the start of their flight in Chicago to break the World Record in marathon flying (1929). 700 hours in the air is the target and their Stinson-Detroit plane "Chicago We Will" can take off as soon as the weather clears.

→ At the Fidelity Coal Mine, near DuQuoin, the – at the time – world's largest stripper type shovel is being used in one of the pits. It is the "Marion Type 5600 electric" and is equipped with a 120-foot boom, 84 foot dipper handle and a 15 cubic yard dipper.

↑ Public Reading Rooms in Chicago where the unemployed can come and read the newspapers free of charge.

← The entire Fidelity Coal Mine, near DuQuoin, is electrified so far as it is economically possible with General Electric Company equipment. This includes all the stripper shovels as well as the leading shovels, tipple, etc. The photograph shows the machinery and spool for winding the 2 $1/8$ inch cable that handles the dipper on the "Marion Type 5600 electric" shovel.

Near the shores of Lake Michigan not far from the city's finest district a new neighborhood is founded upon the empty plots of land, where the unemployed recycle refuse and piece together furniture and shelter.

Michigan Avenue dolls up for convention. Looking south on Chicago's famous Michigan Avenue festooned in bunting and flags as part of the decoration on behalf of the Republican convention which opened in the windy city on June 14th, 1932.

↑ Victory celebrations on State Street in 1936. President Franklin D. Roosevelt wins reelection and tens of thousands gather to cheer the news.

→ In 1932 the communist movement was alive and well in the USA, and found strong support in Chicago, as can be seen at this demonstration in Union Square.

The drive to the office will take a little longer today. The record April blizzard of 1938 blanketed Chicago with more than 7 inches of snow.

With full speed ahead this tugboat shlepps its load along the Chicago River before the mounting ice brings it to a full stop. Icy lows from the North bring the river traffic to a standstill almost every winter.

View of the Wrigley Building at break time.

A throwback from earlier times. This old light house was a favorite retreat and meeting place for fishing and makes a stunning contrast to the skyscrapers in the distance.

A local commentator was so enthused by this drawbridge he called it one of the "Seven Modern Wonders of the World". Had he seen the Tower Bridge in London he might have modified his opinion. A steamer heads towards Lake Michigan

↑ This little cargo boat is equipped with ballast tanks. If the river floods it can lie deep in water and continue under bridges without their having to be opened.

→ In 1928 Chicago was still rivaling New York with its highrises and elevated streets. This is a view of the city center from Wacker Drive along Chicago River.

Chicago's Stock Yards return to life. Before the embers of the eight million Dollar Chicago Stock Yards fire had cooled, temporary office buildings were being erected and shipments of cattle were being received. The photo above shows hastily-built sheds for offices, cattle and trains in the yards. In the background the skeleton of the Exchange building.

Gigantic cattle herds at the slaughterhouse area.

↑ The first double tiered highway in the center of Chicago was built at a cost of 20 million dollars. Wacker Drive replaces the old famous Water Street with its vegetable and produce markets. The parade of trucks is part of the official opening ceremonies.

← The most populated and busiest section of the city, Chicago's Jewish district on Maxwell Street in the heart of the city.

In 1924 the traffic situation in Chicago grew to alarming proportions and the call to build a subway system became louder. A new type of street car has made its appearance on the street, which had been especially built for underground transportation.

40 feet below the streets 132 electric locomotives and 3,000 freight cars, with a capacity of one to six tons each, handle so much freight, that 5,000 trucks are taken off the streets. There are no collisions as the trains use their tracks in a one-way system, guarded by block signals. These freight cars are heavily loaded with merchandise, which they discharge at the big department stores and the various mercantile establishments. They are moved by elevators in and out of the tunnel system. The system of tunnels and equipment is owned and operated by the Chicago Tunnel Company.

Already in 1927 parking was an acute problem. The city is logjammed. The hapless commuters of the nation's second largest city have to park their cars in the massive lot at Grant Park. The workers and shoppers park here and walk to work or take public transportation.

↑ Openings onto the river side from the lower level of Wacker Drive offer some light, and a newly discovered parking spot for the chronically overcrowded downtown area.

→ Michigan Avenue with its highrises, department stores, double-decker buses, and pedestrians in 1927. One of Chicago's busiest arteries. Just a hundred years ago this was a small village.

↑ Six-lane traffic over the Chicago River, before the pedestrian was an endangered species. Wide walkways offer enough space for tourists and pedestrians.

→ A typical workday 1926. Every morning the office towers on State Street suck in tens of thousands of employees and spit them out again in the evening. Stress everywhere, on the streets on the sidewalks, in the trams. How much time will be left before the traffic collapses?

A new first! On October 12th, 1926 Chicago's State Street becomes the world's longest street to be completely illuminated. 140 new street lamps, of 2,000 watt capacity each, with an output of 45.000 lumens for each lamp turn the night into day. The lights extend from Lake to Van Buren.

Michigan Avenue, Chicago's main street, seen from the Standard Oil Building.

The view from the Standard Oil Building onto Michigan Avenue and the bridge over the Chicago River offers this impressionable city scape.

A shot taken over Chicago from aboard the "Graf Zeppelin". One can see the curious multitudes gathered on the streets.

In 1933 the famous airship 'Graf Zeppelin' visited the Chicago World's Fair. Here it is landing, the smoke beneath the Zeppelin is produced to show the pilot the direction of the wind.

Dr. Hugo Eckener, commander of the "Graf Zeppelin" being interviewed by reporters after the landing in Chicago on the dirigible. He will be feted at the World's Fair and then proceed by train to Akron to rejoin his ship.

Chicago gets a unique lighting system. Light poles are all dressed up with a funny-looking man holding up a tray. The statues will be formally dedicated by Major Cermak, at which time the contents of the tray may be identified.

The Art Institute of Chicago is well protected by these watchful sculptures, that keep the skyscrapers opposite Michigan Avenue at bay.

The nation's greatest peace time air armada swept out of the North in May, 1931 and "attacked" the city of Chicago during the combined maneuvers of the Army Air Corps. The battle planes streaked fifty miles along the Lake Michigan front in war array from Waukigan to Gary. The heavily armed bombers, speedy pursuit ships, and fighting attack units completely "obliterated" the Windy City and other points in its wake while thousands below looked on helplessly, getting an idea of what might happen to their city should a real war take place. Over 670 planes took part in the maneuvers.

↑ A view along the Chicago lake front where thousands of Chicagoans witnessed in May, 1931 the "destruction" of their beautiful city at the hands of air raiders.

→ This air view gives an indication of the immensity of the blaze which leveled twelve square blocks of Chicago's Stock Yard District. Raging for five hours, the fire resisted the efforts of 1,000 firemen comprising all available companies, destroying homes and business buildings to wreak a damage estimated at $10,000,000. When the flames had been finally subdued a check-up revealed: three firemen burned beyond recognition, scores injured, thousands homeless, and 40 business buildings, among them two banks, reduced to shambles. The conflagration, of unknown origin, started in the sheep-pen of the stockyards, and spread rapidly fanned by a 35mph wind.

Stock Yard District residents picking up the pieces among the ruins of their homes after the fire of 1934.

Air view of gutted Chicago Stock Yards after the catastrophe of the 1934 fire eerily resemble the ravages of war. Halsted Street running left to right, across the middle of the photo. Across the railroad tracks (at top of the picture), the Exchange Building and the cattle pens of the Stock Yard.

Postmaster Genaral opens World Fair. Accompanied by State and city officials, Postmaster General James A. Farley, representing President Roosevelt, rides in the parade which preceded the official opening of the Chicago "Century of Progress Exposition" on May 27th, 1933. Left to right: Farley; Govenor Henry Horner of Illinois; Rufus Dawes, President of the exposition; and Major E. J. Kelly of Chicago.

"The Century of Progress Exposition" was the banner of the 1933 World's Fair. Hundreds of thousands of proud Chicagoans join international visitors to line Michigan Avenue. The photo shows the parade passing down the Avenue of Flags on the Fair Grounds. Thirty thousand had paid admission to the Fair Grounds at this time.

West Point cadets parade at the opening ceremony of the World's Fair, 1933.

↑ The World's Fair expands off-shore. The "Century of Progress" exposition from the air.

→ The sun sets between the two masts of the great sky ride over the fairgrounds.

Powerful floodlights point to the sky above the "Century of Progress Exposition" and onto its buildings and the masts of the sky ride. Daring World's Fair visitors who 'take a lift' with the sky ride will never forget the thrill of travelling through this sypmhony of colored illumination.

94

A Robot, depicting the noted comedian, Fred Allen, in every mannerism, left New York City on the Broadway Limited, May 29th, bound for Chicago and the World's Fair. Willie Marshall, engineer of the Broadway Limited, welcomes the robot as a passenger, while the real Fred Allen (right) is on hand to bid his likeness bon voyage.

Cover Photo (front)   Michigan Avenue, Chicago's main street
Cover Photo (back)   The parade of trucks is part of the opening ceremonies on Wacker Drive,
                      the first double tiered highway in the center of Chicago

All Photographs   Courtesy of:
                      THE INTERNATIONAL HISTORICAL PRESS PHOTO COLLECTION
                      of SWERIGES TELEVISION AB, Stockholm

Introduction   John Hartray

Reproductions   Repro-Team GmbH, Weingarten
Printing and Binding Druck- und Verlagshaus Erfurt seit 1948, GmbH, Erfurt
Cover Design   Julie von der Ropp

Printed in Germany